MY JACKDAW DAYS AND CORVID WAYS

MY JACKDAW DAYS AND CORVID WAYS

JAMES DONALDSON

My Jackdaw Days and Corvid Ways
James Donaldson

INTRODUCTION

I have always felt impelled to write, poetry has been my way of
exploring and resolving, as much as it can, my past. Acting as
a mirror, reflecting the shadows and light that compose being.
In these poems, the Jackdaw emerges as my alter ego, a figure
that has haunted my life, much as he inhabits these verses. He is
my sometime confidant, sometime friend, and sometime critic, a
presence that reflects my own uncertainties and inner darkness.

This book is divided into two parts, the first consists of twenty-
three poems inviting readers into a landscape steeped in
melancholy, where Jackdaws, Ravens, and other birds occasionally
intervene, metaphors for loss, longing, and the beauty found
in life's darker moments. These poems draw on the enigmatic
nature of these birds to explore themes of solitude, mystery, and
resilience.

The second part consists of three "dialogues", in which I bring
together characters who have always fascinated me, voices from
literature, history, and myth, to let them speak to each other in
ways I wish they could. These conversations became a space to
explore questions I often ask myself about love, power, morality,
and the stories we tell to make sense of the world. They blur the
lines between history, myth, and fiction, allowing voices from
different worlds to meet, clash, and possibly harmonise.

This collection is, in many ways, a reflection of my inner
landscape, its shadows and light, its quiet moments and wild
imaginings. I hope you find in these pages something that resonates
with your own experiences, whether in the rustle of a Jackdaw's
wings or the murmur of a dialogue that might never have been.

ACKNOWLEDGMENT

To Anna-Marie Buss, artist, partner and friend, my love and infinite thanks for the stunning illustrations that grace the pages of this collection. Your artistry breathes life into the words, that enhances the poem's emotional intention.

I am truly in awe of your talent and vision, which so beautifully complement and elevate the poetry within. Thank you for sharing your brilliance and for bringing this book to life with your flawless work. Thank you also for helping me negotiate the maze of editing and preparation for publication...   I love you

DEDICATION

From the man at the window table, with too many pens, and far too many sheets of paper! This collection, My Jackdaw Days and Corvid Ways, is dedicated to the unfailingly friendly staff and the baristas at Black Sheep Coffee in Tunbridge Wells, and Finch House in Tonbridge. Thank you for your patience, kindness, encouragement and interest. And of course, the excellent coffee! All of which were essential in the creation of this collection. My grateful thanks to you all.

"One more cup of coffee before I go..." (Bob Dylan)

CONTENTS

POEMS

DIALOGUES

MY JACKDAW DAYS, AND CORVID WAYS

PART I

My Jackdaw days were never golden,
they were oil-slick light
and whisper thin.
Stitched together with copper wire and
an unforgiving easterly wind,
more glint than gleam.
I wore my feathers for all to see
like a thief wears his unquiet silence,
gathering bright things I couldn't keep,
a key, a lie, a laugh, too late.
Everything that was almost mine.

I moved through my hours sideways,
head tilted towards the forgotten.
The sky spoke slowly in riddles,
I answered in echoes.
Cousin crows preached from rooftops,
I listened like a disciple,
waiting for a sermon,
that might name me friend.

My corvid ways were always crooked truths,
small violence of an untamed spirit.
I never sang so sweetly,
but knew the tunes of leaving.
Arias I learned but never earned
still twitch in my bones.
I followed the blueprint of flight
across the sky.
I don't understand gravity,
I just defy it daily.
On hopeless days
I rested in the rafters of neglect,
calling down to passing lovers
who lose themselves in smoke.

On other days
I'd disappear
into the ink of my own shadow.
Watching the world
through a glimmer of ill-gotten glass
…darkly.
But these were not my glory days,
they were scavenged.
Sewn together from broken promises
that were all mine... all that I owned.

My Jackdaw days and corvid ways.
I carry them still,
quiet in my chest.
A feather caught
in the throat of unmelodious birdsong.

PART II

I have lived in the gleam of guttered things,
found silver in the wreckage,
found laughter in cracked discarded bones.
I was not built for the banquet,
I took my crumbs from windowsills.

These are my Jackdaw days,
bright-eyed in the dark.
Hoarding the shine that no one wants,
a broken watch-face,
a key to no door,
a name whispered hoarsely.
Whispered often.

I learned to love
the shimmer of almost,
the rusted edges of maybe.
I built my home from glances,
from misfit hymns,
from the silence that ensued
when the truth had nothing to add.

My corvid ways.
I won't forget,
not the hands that fed me stones,
not the sky that closed its mouth
when I begged for light.
But I must forgive,
as a bird forgives the wind
for defying it …again, and again.

Now, I only speak in clicks,
in shadows,
in riddles tied to feathers,
in unfinished sentences.
Don't ask me for cleaner lines
or a straighter way.
I only sing in circles.
I only love in detours.

Still.
I've seen the world from a wire,
seen the ruin,
and though it isn't always kind,
it is sometimes beautiful,
sometimes misrepresented.
Like a mirror,
cracked into constellations
crazed as confused paving.

These are my Jackdaw days.
These are my corvid ways,
and they will carry me
when wings remember
what hearts have lost.

THE YEAR ROUND

I SPRING:

Stirred by the violet's first uncertain bloom
April whispers its sunrise song
The earth rouses, pregnant with matriarchal memory
As if the slow thawing soil calls back to mind
Footprints of long-departed souls
And in the ever-expanding light
Shadows contract
And the heart, attuned to impending heat
Finds renewal, forswearing bitter winter's melancholy

II SUMMER:

Beneath the oppressive brilliance of noontide
The gardener's delight wilts, heavy with eloquent scent
Extravagant roses shed petals like silent regrets
Scattering them like fragrant snowflakes
Upon the now parched perfumed ground
The air, thick with scent, and the hum of insistent insect wings
Presses upon my hot and weary soul
Untimely reminders, that even in its fullness
There lurk the seeds of inevitable decline

III AUTUMN:

A cold indifferent wind stalks the lately stubbled fields
Exuding the consoling aroma of distant fires
Leaves, chilled, brittle and resigned
Descend in leisurely spirals
Gold, red and amber, testament to the years decent
The veiled horizon, a tapestry of dramatic hues
Foretells closure
And the soul, wrapped in the winding-sheet of nostalgia
Reckons its losses with melancholic reverence

IV WINTER:

In the stillness and utter silence of frost-bound days
Time faulters, congeals and gives pause
Skeletal trees, etched against an arctic pewter sky
Stand monument to forlorn absence
Footsteps misplaced in the snow's numbing hush
Fade, leaving not a trace behind
And yet, beneath the bleached and baren blanket, snow
The faintest pulse persists undaunted
An almost imperceptible promise of hope
Confident, awaiting the returning sun

THE PIGEON AND THE OWL

Somewhere, between the pigeon and the owl
Unable to turn back life's relentless clock
I lose my way
A precocious moron floundering
Foundering on the rock of regret
And marvelling at my infinite capacity for folly
Somewhere, between the owl and the pigeon
Between pointless pessimism, and imprudent optimism

Sometime, between the first thought and the last word
The dreaming pigeon's fancy turns to love
Once more astray
In foolish fantasy's pursuit
The collared dove, to press his suit
Aimless, hopeless, helpless, failing, falling short
Somehow unable to find the courage, eyes open, to leap into the abyss
To discover what it would feel like, love's first kiss

Somehow, between delusion and logic's cold, inevitable conclusion
The egotist owl sits motionless
Overthinking's frozen prey
With daytime, night-time, nightmare vision
Unable to process or progress a decision
A child's mind in an adult's body, desire's victim
Sometime before time itself, running ever faster, runs out
Leaving me stranded, left to shake a disappointed fist and shout

THE IMPOSTER'S TALE

I came to town under a borrowed name
A second-hand story, a fistful of shame
Nobody asked, "from whence I came?"
I'll let the night decide
A teacher sought out love and sin
The preacher taught that I can't win
But what they said just kept me thin
I'll let the night decide

An angel touched my face and heart
I kissed her hand, I played my part
I could always end, but never start
I'll let the night decide
Cards got dealt, and dice got thrown
The debt I ran cut to the bone
The house can't lose, it's made of stone
I'll let the night decide

I hear the wind sing songs I know
Forgotten tunes of long ago
I can't stay and I can't go
I'll let the night decide
The mirror cracked as years went past
In the role I played, I was miscast
I smiled too slow, and spoke too fast
I'll let the night decide

I thought I knew myself full well
But truth be told I couldn't tell
If I was sick or I was well
I'll let the night decide
I'm here at last in borrowed skin
A stranger looks out from within
An impostor's face fixed with a grin
I daren't let the night decide

REMEMBRANCE

Out of nothing something comes
Into nowhere something goes

Lately I've been pondering,
the "if" of remembrance,
"if" indeed, there will be an "if" at all,
as "if" that could truly matter to anyone but me.
And "if" so, how might that "if" be?
The "if" that lies at the heart of life itself,
will necessarily be,
as seen by an indifferent universe, transitory...
So much less than fractional,
indeed, less than the lifespan of a virtual particle.
Insignificant, unregistered, unregistering,
either returning from an indisputable future,
or advancing from an uncertain past.
(Thank you for that thought Mr Feynman!)

"Ifs", found also in strife, and adrift,
 perceived by an individual, who is forever looking up and out.
From a life which can feel, in any given moment, unbearable,
or occasionally, paradoxically, endless,
as, at the same time, it passes too terrifyingly swiftly.
Life, the incidental outcome
of an accidental collaboration.
A triumph of the fastest swimmer, beating the odds.
Giving rise to a lifetime of hows, but never moment of whys.
Whilst occasioning the subordinate wheres, and whens.

The how, itself a tale of infinite interactions,
emotional reactions to random chance events,
that, in turn, circumscribe and circumvent
the happenstance of human commerce.
With friends, enemies, lovers, and strangers,
appearing then disappearing in turn, without warning.
Endlessly changing places,
exchanging faces, in the how and the now.

What might I say, to these actors,
In their cloud-capp'd towers, gorgeous palaces, and solemn temples.
What can I say, about a globe,
inhabited, imagined, or falsely glimpsed?
What might I say, of a life so carelessly lived?
"Just that I must betray you all by forgetting you,
as surely you will forget me".
I pray therefore, "forgive my forgetting,
as I forgive, in advance, yours".
Before the final "if" of that long, oft longed for sleep.

Ex quidem nihil fit
Nusquam aliquid vadit in

BLACK BIRD

The black bird,
camouflaged in modest melancholy.
Childhood's conjoined companion alights,
my seductive siren, inner voice.
Extinguishing, in an instant, joy and hope.
Inviting me, enticing me, to dive,
submerge and never resurface.
Unbidden… inevitable… unavoidable...
Depression's invisible event horizon crossed once more,
the irresistible pull of an emotional black hole,
yawns and swallows me whole…
Time slows.

Desolation, clothed in familiar garb,
as familiar as my witch mother's sable cat,
as suffocating as a mummy's bandages.
Arrives coffin swaddled
in innumerable shades of darkness.
Self-indulgent avian usurer
occasioned by conscious and unconscious memory.
Childhood's nightmares.
The cynical crash of hatred's symphony number 9,
heard through fractured malleus, incus, and stapes.

A dissonant musical rendition of maternal love, long dead.
Of desiccated passion turned to frostbitten hatred,
as dry as an Antarctic winter,
as cold as a summer night in the desert.
Composed for violin, viola and violence.
Performed for broken hearts, broken promises,
and broken dreams.
To a chorus of shattered crockery, on porcelain days,
on fragmented terracotta afternoons,
and splintered China nights.

Unrelenting belligerents, locked in mortal combat
blind to the world in their fury.
Deceived, believing no one else can hear
the incessant din of your internecine war.
Your Pyrrhic victory immortalised
in the collateral damage of lost innocence.
An opus sure to conjure the sombre raven,
my lifelong companion.
A bleak beaked black bird on a bleak black background,
feathered ebony wraith, legendary hraefn.
Summoned from some ancient,
cursed, forgotten, Saxon barrow
whose cyclical cynical voice, croaking almost imperceptibly
whispers the hopeless choice of being.

CURIOUS ABOUT THE STRANGE EXPERIENCE CALLED LIFE

PART I WAKING

The morning illuminates my reluctant eyelids,
an incoming tide of light and surplus obligation.
Somewhere a distant a bird sings,
a melody too perfect to be true.
Enslaved, I reach for my phone,
my tether to the universe's perpetual insistence.
The awakening sky conjures a question,
"wasn't I meant to be something today?"

PART II MID-MORNING

Hours blur, like a watercolour in the rain,
blue as a threatening email, red as a siren sunset.
Green for the strangers who rush and brush past,
not caring to know my name.
Hiding, camouflaged in sorrow I forget to breathe,
until my coffee finally grows cold.
Outside a rebellious wind stirs without my consent,
I should pay better attention?
But the world is a slippery beast,
always mocking, remaining just beyond my reach.

PART III FADING

Paused, by the inexorable weight of quiet moments,
static and the streetlights flicker into life.
Out of sight a child laughs without reason,
and the moon appears, too soon, far too soon.
An uninvited guest in a late afternoon sky.
Intrigued, I wonder, pondering, does it watch me
in the same way I stare at my reflection?
Curious… distant… uncertain…

PART IV DARKENING

Night settles at last, like a relieving sigh,
staring up at a blank canvas, my ever-patient ceiling.
The surface, on which my inconclusive thoughts refuse to settle.
Somewhere someone is trying to hold on.
Somewhere someone is trying to let go.
Somewhere someone is being born, slowly.
Somewhere someone is dying, quickly.
In this ever-evolving landscape of reflection,
I remind myself, "this is all there is"
I ask myself, "is this all there is?"
My strange, as yet unfinished story means,
that I'm too busy to begin to understand.

MR POE'S RAVEN

Mr Poe's raven, forevermore cursed
Bird of ill omen, invoked in your verse
A bird black as mourning, a bird clothed in sable
A bird for all seasons, a bird from a fable
Avian harbinger, herald of death
Perch now upon my shoulder
    to share my last breath.

Invisible companion, you fill empty space
You move me tears, there's no joy on your face
Scream like poor Munch, at the noise and the pain
Of the chattering pollution, where none dare take the blame

No footprint, no fortune, no time to forget
In the fog of confusion, live a life of regret
Fly past my window, a ghost in the night
Your corax shaped shadow, corrupting my sight

A home fit for heroes, all promises are broken
In a mirage of meaning, words best left unspoken
Unwelcome as Banquo, not the last or the least
Unsatisfied hunger, blighting the feast

Mr Poe's raven, forevermore cursed
Bird of ill omen, invoked in your verse
A bird black as mourning, a bird clothed in sable
A bird for all seasons, a bird out of a fable
Avian harbinger, herald of death
Perch now upon my shoulder
    to share my last breath.

SEASONS

An ancient man in a sorrowful winter coat
A sorrowful man in an ancient winter coat
Threadbare, with a stumbling gait

Gelid feet in long decaying summer shoes
Walking streets of long forgotten summer heat
Invisible, shambling towards your inevitable fate

A grey-haired man, in subtle autumn colours
An autumn man subdued by falling leaves
Discarded, soon to be no more

Springtime memories, evoking rheumy tears
Salt-streaked cheeks, one time home to spring's kisses
Now obsolete, broken, washed-up on life's uncertain shore

An ancient man in a sorrowful winter coat
A sorrowful man in an ancient winter coat
Threadbare, with a stumbling gait

STRAP-HANGING, NORTH
OF MOORGATE

Adrift again, beneath a network of vanished streets
strap-hanging, north of Moorgate.
Sickly sodium light blurs the faces of weary strangers,
who exchanged winter's glacial dangers
for uncertain subterranean sanctuary.

Custom demands reticence.
Reserve must, after all, preserve a shrunken personal place,
a sacred space not to be invaded.
I withdraw, tasting the labyrinth's ionised breath.
Hardly a presence, I persist upon the platform.
Subdued but displaying appropriate indifferent fortitude.
A cacophonous din, and blast of hot air,
sirocco, fit to melt the face but not the heart.
Heralds the impatiently awaited carriages arrival.
Multiple mouths open as one,
quickly consuming the hustling host,
commuters compete for a vacant seat,
as doors close mindfully,
encapsulating us in close company.

The metal snake heaves,
sighing between station stops.
Steel pulses beneath the never sleeping city's tired bones.
Strangers mutter mantras behind backlit screens,
fixated on fiction, murder, or love's lost dreams.
Neon syllables stutter, reflecting on grimy windows.
(Efficiency's inevitable though unintended outcome.)

Riding the rails,
ingenuities imagination realised
in steel and stone.
A place, the space where imagination wonders,
and polite private eyes won't make unwanted contact.
Even so sly glances will still take their chances,
and go pursuing beauty (two seats down and across.)
Igniting a never to be fulfilled fantasy, my loss.
And so it is,
an uninvited, unintended internal dialogue begins.

"She wasn't there yesterday
Might she be there tomorrow?
More lust than love,
More doubt than sorrow

And would I have the nerve, and dare to speak?
Or would I even know the words to choose?
To risk rebuff, and chance to lose
Would I break the unwritten law of silence?...

I think not

And would you if you knew me
Dain to meet?
Upon some foreign shore or wind-swept street
Would you, could you, spot me in a crowd
Fulfil my dream, speak my name out loud"

Passing over uneven points I'm jolted back
to the uninspiring present.
Breaking the self-indulgent chain
of meandering rambling thought.
My would be, could be,
dream assignation with Aphrodite dissipates.
And once again, I notice the stale smell.
olfactory ghost,
reminder of soot choked tunnels.

Slowing to a stop (Chalk Farm past!)
Before the hushed release
of furtive sliding doors which open
to disgorge the home-bound hordes.
Among whom,
my minds-eye goddess, rises to depart.
And unwitting, tears a fragment from my heart.

I'm left standing, hanging on, whilst letting go.
It wasn't real, I tell myself, I know.
The doors close,
shutting out my hope.
My cryptic face no hint of loss will ever show,
my mind turns in, just two more stops to go.

"She wasn't there yesterday
Might she be there tomorrow?
More lust than love,
More doubt than sorrow"

A PIGEON ON A COLD PARK BENCH

A pigeon perches on a cold park bench
Feathers puffed out
Fighting the winter's bitter cold
Gray and oil-slick iridescent
In January's meagre light

Sitting with the certainty of an ancient stone
Monument to stillness

A stranger, frozen mid-step
Is transfixed by the pigeon's unblinking eye
A fragment of shared silence
Hanging like a question mark between them
And for the merest moment
The universe pauses
The traffic's din dies
And the razor-sharp whistle of the wind
Is turned speechless

A bird, a stranger
And the imperceptible fragile thread of being
That momentarily unites them
In this place, this time

The pigeon cocks its head, as if to ask
"What brought you here"?

The stranger, hands buried deep in his pockets
Offers nothing but his presence in response...
Then walks on

The pigeon remains
Its life heavy with the weight of the moment
Waiting perhaps, for the next stranger...

SISTER BROTHER

Sister brother, absent mother
Father fled, replaced by lover
Born by chance, no love's devotion
Abandoned freely, without emotion
Nights in terror, screams resounding
Washed-out days, all fear confounding
Book companions, last redoubt
Between the pages, my way out

Time passed slowly, cold confusion
Loving family, ideal's illusion
Crisis climax, siblings scattered
Linger lonely, last hope shattered
Chest constricting, hardly breathing
Let me go now, no one grieving
Burned out, broken, beyond redeeming
Doomed to distance, hopeless dreaming

Cursed unfeeling, not connecting
Unquenched desire, love disrespecting
Swift to anger, slow to reason
If no one's friend, there can't be treason
Sister brother, you understand
That feeling's merely contraband
Wasted years, old pain, and sorrow
Unfit for love, unkind tomorrow

Don't speak to me of kindred's ties
False spoken love and other lies
I trust no body, let no one in
No parasite beneath my skin
A lesson learned in childhood days
That closeness hoodwinks and betrays
No sacred calling, to be mother
But for my sister and my brother

JESTER'S SONG

An indifferent winter's day dawns,
February, crystal cold encroaches.
Stepping out, unconfident, from a grey unsuitable door.
The treacherous ice-bound pavement awaits.

Unbidden, inevitable,
My Jackdaw jester, unfaithful companion comes calling,
Folding silent spectral sable wings,
He begins to sing his sixpenny song.

"Dead, not dead, long gone away,
Pain began and slow decay.
Love gone so long, recalled to mind.
Too easy lost, so hard to find.
Engulfed in need, your time of sorrow,
Forget today, reminisce tomorrow.

Lost, not lost, you can't forget,
The scent of hair, the taste of sweat.
A voice to set, one's heart afire,
To fill your heart, ignite desire.
And fifty years, will not suffice,
To quench your thirst, turn love to ice.

Long, too long, enough you cry,
Seek peace of mind before you die.
Now let her go, leave her to rest,
The dream was doomed, could ne'er be blessed.
All love since then, flawed by regret,
Just shadow love, loves silhouette."

Song sung, song done, a tragic tale of woe,
Song done, song sung, the hoarse tones of a crow,
Song sung, song done, Jack its time to go.

AGORAPHOBIC NIGHTMARE

Walking fast,
Step… step… step

My defensive rhythm,
Fast enough to outpace the shoelaced strangers
Dangers robed in human form
Step… step… step

Weaving my web of invisible distance
Maintaining safe space
Between the I and the suffocating, agitating
Hoard of alien shapeshifters
That surround and threaten to drown me
Step… step… step

Maintain too a morning face
Designed to match my pace
Chosen with care, inscrutable, insubstantial, forgettable
Don't stare, don't dare,
And whatever I do
Don't snare the haunted eyes of the grief grassed wraiths
As they scurry, hurry, and worry their way to their
unwelcome work
Step… step… step

Ambition… to be invisible
To that end hat pulled down, and looking down
Always looking down
Step… step… step

Glancing up, only occasionally,
To confirm the safety of separation
But avoid the eyes of the ghosts
Whose false alibis of feeling
Are etched on faces of mock sorrow
Step... step... step

Tripping on a broken flagstone
My streetwalking, sleepwalking spell shattered
My mantle of concealment lost
Clock dial, crocodile countenances turn towards me
Raptor senses tuned to measure movement
Seek out the tumbling, stumbling, bumbling dunce
That I have suddenly unwittingly become
Fall down, guilty frown, clown face
Clown shoes, short fuse,
Rise irate, bereft of grace
Change direction run for cover
Break the rhythm
Step... step... step... step... step

Duck down an inconvenient alley
Slow down... breathe... breathe
Out of sight of mocking eyes
Arrest my flight and,
Reset the beat of clown clothed feet
And curse my costly, loss of concentration
Step... step... step...

Diverted now
My routine mournful morning course forsaken
A new route must be taken
My agoraphobic nightmare come to pass
Reflected in the glass
Of vacant shops and passing cars
Whose numbers are unknown to me
Unfamiliar places, unfamiliar spectral faces
Hat down, head down,
Head downtown
My weaving dancer's feet
Pick up the beat
Step... step... step

Slow my breathing,
Calm my mind
Multiply by seventeens
Avoid the cracks, step between
Step... 561... step... 578... step... 595... step... 612

Reset my compass,
To quell the rising panic
Steer homeward if I can
816... 833... 850... step

Duck, dodge, weave believe I can
Elude the haunting hunting eyes
Of rat face, rat race swarming spies
In unbecoming, ugly mortal guise
Who wait each time I step outside
1,003… step

Second left, step… step… step…
Third right 1,343... step…

Home safe at last,
Door closed, locked fast
A wooden bulwark interposed
Before my last redoubt
My hideout from
A universe of phantoms
Both unseen and seen
That haunt my waking dreams
And would devour me.

THE POET AND THE LOVER'S CHOICE

PART I, THE POET'S CHOICE

The page grows cold, but still, it sings
A melody that love once knew
It echoes deep, but silent clings
To all that time and pain accrue
The poet speaks, though love has died
    ... *"Can verse alone be satisfied?"*

She walked away, and yet she stayed
Within the prison of my rhyme
A love now lost; a heart betrayed
Yet ink still traps her form in time
She fades in life, but lives in art
    ... *"Which truth holds the greater part?"*

Her touch a dream, turned startling pale
Though words remain where flesh must wane
Can ink, where memory's doomed to fail
Restore the warmth once known in vain
A lover's arms, a poet's quill
    ... *"Which emptiness, is emptier still?"*

The poet's love, the lover's muse
One captive, one forever free
Yet love, once found, one must refuse
For art demands its loyalty
The heart must choose its hollowed throne
    ... *"To reign with words, or love unknown?"*

She calls no more, nor speaks my name
Yet every line still breathes her face
Does poetry preserve the flame
Or mock the warmth it can't replace?
To love in life or love in lore?
    ... *"Which grief is worse? Which haunts us more?"*

And so, the choice is made at last
The lover lost; the poet won
Yet ever words recalls the past
The tale unwritten, left undone
To write of love, and know its cost
    ... *"Does the poet gain, when love is lost?"*

THE POET AND THE LOVER'S CHOICE

PART II, THE LOVER'S CHOICE

Upon some page her voice is caught
Each whispered song, a midnight air
Each line a thread of longing wrought
A secret woven, soft and rare
Yet love, though penned with unsound art
   ..."*Could it ever tame the beating heart?*"

He traced her name in trembling ink
A vow on every fumbling line
Yet love in words begins to sink
A shadow cast by fate's design
To write of love, to feel it burn
   ..."*Which path to choose? Which road to run?*"

For poetry, the soul must bleed
Its fire consuming all it finds,
Yet love untamed, will plant new seed
To bloom beyond the poet's mind
The fleeting touch of loves first kiss
   ..."*Can verse replace the bliss of this?*"

Her lips like petals, soft, unfold
Her breath the warmth of coming dawn
Yet ink, more steadfast, sure as gold
Remains when transient youth is gone
Love or verse, one fades one stays
    …"Which will endure? Which wane away?"

To love, to write, two paths diverge
One passing, one in death remains
Yet love's own voice might quell the urge
To trade her scope for poets' chains
A lovers' arms, a poet's soul
    …"Can one embrace, yet not be whole?"

She calls, and so the pages weep
Of lovers' warmth, or words embrace
To live, to love to dream, to keep
What sacrifice, what choice to face?
Between her lips and lines of art
    …"The poet yields his longing heart?"

THE MASTER AND HIS EMISSARY:
THE MYSTERY OF MIND

The Master persists in the hollow places,
among shadows of cedars and ancient memory.
The Emissary moves,
fast as a photon in a vacuum.
We walk, puppets at their bidding,
counting endless steps on the paths they pave.
Paths to nowhere, while they watch,
from the folds in their white and grey clouds.
From the electric byways that channel thought.

They exist inseparable, twin stars fettered,
illuminating my inner universe.
Speaking wordless, the original language of instinct.
Castor and Pollux, paradox of eternally fractured grace.
Locked in the enduring struggle between reason and emotion,
where music is the vocabulary of wisdom,
and speech, the nonsense uttered to fill the void.

"Measure! Measure! The Emissary cries
in his world of parts.
Where the whole divides,
Where no measure made
may fathom the tide.
Where unseen currents of thought reside
Where the Master laughs, his tranquil chime
resonant as the sweep of time"

Between them pulses the silent chord.
Left, hemisphere of numbers.
Right, a discourse of dreams.
The bridge between,
stretched taut, unseen,
threading logic,
knitting ineffable streams.

In the corridors of grey, the left-side winds
a labyrinth of reason as soft as steel.
But where it goes, and what it finds
is the mystery of being; the enigma that is mind.

The right-side murmurs, belief's refrain.
The song of life.
Mapping out an atlas in a mist of images,
arising to overwhelm and frame
the frontiers that forever wax and wane,
between the ache of pleasure, and the joy of pain.

Time is tolled in pulsing rhythms of thought,
dissolving in the swell, the ebb and flow of light.
Paths converge, and for a second love is caught,
judgement overthrown; faculty come to naught.
Where whispered words of wisdom can't be thought.

The tough body,
where two rivers, left and right collide.
Where mind becomes memory,
and memories reside.
The conjunction of the sacred and profane,
the seat of self, the subject unexplained.

"The Emissary's reign begins to fade,
light retreats before advancing shade.
As the world, at last, grown still and dim,
the Master's song, the final hymn."

AN ODE TO BOB, CHANGING TIMES

Bob with woven words and music
And the superhuman crew
Held at bay the Hard Rain
Untangled days so blue
A Sad Eyed Lady's love song
Her lover's words entwined
The Tambourine Mans Laughter
Still echoes in my mind

To escape the Jokers watchtower
And Frankie Lee's last leap
I drank One More Cup Of Coffee
And dreamt of Mozambique
Awoken by the ticking clock
I knew I was too late
The blind man's parrot cried aloud
A tale of twisted fate

Queens Anne and Jane seduced me
Kept me up beyond the dawn
In Cold Iron Bound I found myself
Lost, lovesick and forlorn
In time your Chimes of Freedom
Released me from my fears
Of penny-whistle rainbows
And Calypso singers fears

Down Desolations highway
With Einstein in disguise
To jingle jangle music
I danced to my surprise
Starry eyed and laughing
I Sheltered From The Storm
Of broken ploughs and broken vows
And Mona Lisa's scorn

I busted out the basement
Then fled to Maggie's Farm
With a silent seasick sailor
Who took me by the arm
Past statues made of matchsticks
In time at last to see
Reflected in a mirror
A ghost that looked like me

From childhood's murmured promise
To shadows falling fast
You comfort and confront me
With words that will outlast
No Motopsycho Nightmare
Will haunt me or upset
The roads still left to travel
Singing, not dark yet.

INVITATION, THE JACKDAW'S SIREN SONG

My sometime unreliable conscience.
The sable swathed Jackdaw clown intrudes,
once more.
Cracking his all too familiar crooked smile.
Dropping his daily mushroom offering,
unsettling my concentration.
A coarsely whispered invitation
to 'abandon yourself to too familiar daydreams.'

Dreams stoic.
I can bear the pain of love and loss.

Dreams heroic.
I can bend the world to my better purpose.

Dreams Homeric.
I can bring life to its necessary melancholic conclusion.

The daydreamers poppy scented path to cognitive oblivion.
Numbing, addictive, seductive.
The beguiling thief of time and action.
Ego, and self-delusion,
writ large upon my time scarred heart.

'Come with me!' Your irresistible corvid consonants cry.
Suffer no longer in silence, explore joy, and sorrow,
paradoxical sides of life's soon spent coinage.
Leave the confines of your histories' limited imagination,
stray outside beleaguered walls of wilful ignorance.

Follow me! follow me!
An exhortation to dance.
Mind at last unlaced.
Explore mycelium nurtured memories,
in psilocybin reverence of other dimensions.
Where there be oracular dragons, unbiddable unicorns,
and a silent ocean, filled with eternally lamenting fish,
unaware of the water they inhabit.
Depart your lamenting longshore empire,
where all are forced, against their will,
to fulfil empty promises.
And bear the blame of previous generations.

VIENNA DREAMS, MACON SCHEMES
A Conversation

(MOZART)
I wrote for Kings, I wrote for Queens
But when the night would steal my breath
I weave my themes that whisper death
It wasn't lace, it wasn't gold
Just my voice, so sad, so cold
Tell me Willie, tell me true
"Did music really unchain you?"

(WILLIE MCTELL)
I walked this world with my guitar spine
A beggar's soul, a voice like wine
I played for dimes, I played for pain
I played for the love that never came
You wrote your notes so clean, so fine
But brother ain't we both gone blind
So tell me now, *"What's left to choose*
When all you got is play or lose?"

(BOTH)
So, strike that key, bend that note
ride that tune like a sinking boat
One was gold, one was blue
But the same old song just runs right through
Yes, the same old song just runs right through

(MOZART)
I woke up drunk in gilded halls
Candles burning, shadows tall
My hands still dance, though I am gone
Playing tunes no man should own
They called me genius, called me damned
But all I was, was a hired hand
Please tell me now, old man in blue
"Does the devil ever talk to you?"

(WILLIE MCTELL)

Oh, I heard your tunes in Macon town
Where the river runs, and the sun beats down
A man can play, but the world plays mean
And I see things you ain't never seen
You had your courts, your powdered wigs
I had the blues and broken strings
But tell me friend, *"What's fame to do*
When the devil's walking next to you?"

(BOTH)

A song's a ghost, a song's a curse
a diamond tune, a hollow verse.
Play it soft, play it loud
It lifts you up, it drags you down
But once you've heard that lonesome sound
You're just some shadow on the ground
So, strike that key, bend that note
ride the tune like a sinking boat
One was gold, one was blue
But the same old song just runs right through
Yes, the same old song just runs right through

EMBANKMENT TO WOODSIDE PARK

Autumn fog persists,
Painting an already mournful sky obscure.
Sad as a cold Ash Wednesday morning.
Asking "what is possible, now… on my journey"?
(If only I could see… clearly!)

Autumn mist insists,
invading pavement cracks and hidden corners,
dark as the widow's mourning weeds.
Questioning "what might yet be possible, soon… as I wonder"?
(If only I believed… truly!)

Autumn mirk resists,
refusing the distant sun's seductive charm.
White as an un-melted January frost.
Enquiring "what was once possible… in some previous life"?
(If only I'd tried… honestly!)

Possibilities, present, future and past,
asked, not answered.
Between Embankment and Woodside Park
an almost empty ghost train transports me,
rattling out its pathetic mantra.
"Never go there… never go there… never go there…"

Spellbound this wretched lonely rider dreams.
Haunted by missed kisses, taunted by lost lovers.
Daunted by the cost of broken promises,
and the echoing remains of long-gone Sunday revellers
reciting their crapulent chorus.
"Drink with me… drink to me… drink to be"

Shut them out! Block them out! Keep them out!
Eclipse the din of bygone vagrant voices,
recite instead, inside your head,
tales of the wretched dead.
Sad stories of the death of Kings
and other things that come to mind,
to blind my ears and bind my eyes in silence.

Doors slide open, issuing a challenge,
to "mind the gap".
To alight on unfamiliar ground,
or stay and dare the eyes of reckless strangers.
Unmoving, the doors close,
and the mantra begins again "never go there…"

THE CORVID CHORUS

"But you don't know what it is"

There aren't many December days
When a sickly sceptic sun troubles itself
Enough to rise above my fractured horizon
Provoking a marginal change in light
Silhouetting the frost shrouded skeletal winter treetops
White against the grey

A provocation, sufficient, to stir my only friend
The crepuscular corvid
Into life and song
A raucous chorus, just enough to rouse me
From my uneasy hibernal sleep
Forcing me to embrace another soulless winter's day

The melancholic ballad
An epic tale of all too familiar failure
A tuneless chanted narrative
Parable of the hapless, thoughtless, faceless
But convincingly cadaverous, Mr Jones
Professor, possessor of a pencil and a confused Bactrian frown
Whose comprehensive library for the illiterate
Couldn't help him find his own way home
Or stop me seeing myself in the mirror of his song

I CAN'T THINK OF ANYTHING WORSE

I really can't think of anything worse
Than listening to someone else's verse
The ponderous unfurling of personal pain
Like watching paint drying in the rain

He clears his throat, she sets the stage
They warn "this comes from a difficult age"
I nod, as if I really care
Whilst wishing I were away somewhere

Metaphors stretch, their stanzas sprawl
(They rhyme Nepal with worn out shawl)
A tragic tale of love grown cold
I think that's what I've just been told

The pauses come, with heartfelt sighs
They wait for tears that no one cries
Applause at last, polite and terse
I really can't think of anything worse

TODAY, AGAIN

A.M. TODAY

Waking to the numerous… far too numerous
Oft regrettable, insatiable, problematic
Elements that comprise and compromise
The stranger I have become
The stranger who appears without fail, in my morning mirror
Staring back,
Now, blessedly short sighted
In hapless, hopeless remembrance of time flown so quickly.

Another day started… startles me
Sometimes possessed…
The Horla
Sometimes unshipped.
Escaping once more to take the stage
An incurably crestfallen romantic Jackdaw
Double chinned, double dealing
Superstitious super spreader
Of life's inevitable disappointments.

Don't dare to dream anymore
Or … do I dare one more day?
Alongside my jet-black nightcap
Flashback, throwback avian confidante
Fabled sign of no one's zodiac but my own.

In company we wend our way
And bend our day to no other purpose
Than to keep a broken promise.

Where to, and how to explore and explain
All my past and current conceits and confusions.
Even as my footsore, Jackdaw alter ego crony
Bolts for the backdoor
Leaving me washed up, screaming
'Am not Prince Hamlet, nor was meant to be!'
On some unfamiliar shore
That does not lead to Elsinore.
Or any other Kingdom that won't be mine.

Onward, if needs must, and time allows
Without the dratted bird
I am sure I can manage just one more day
It's what I have to say
It enables me to linger,
And point an accusing finger
At a world I don't trust... Don't duly, fully, truly believe in.

P.M.

In the afternoon take a lover... if she'll have me
Discover, if just a fraction of that particular satisfaction
Is enough distraction to disremembering
Or does my Swiss cheese brain freeze
At the very thought of intimacy?
Nevertheless, drawn inevitably, irresistibly
Like a moth to the incandescence
Of the beauty that is your face... your form... your thighs
I sigh and know you are my Achilles heel
I can no more resist the urge to merge with you
Than the scorpion can refrain from stinging the frog
Love's fundamental, self-destructive essence
It's in my nature, that's my excuse
Surely better then to remain a recluse,
Than to seduce or be seduced again.

And so, at last to the question
Am I incapable of the necessary honesty?
Another kind of dare maybe
Too scared to share, too scarred to care
Too many questions and no suggestion
Of what answer I might fix upon.

Late afternoon retreats
In need now of diversion I open books
My oldest, dearest friends... endless possibilities
A literary excursion to the intact ideas of better minds
Socrates, inquisitor, corrupter of Athenian youth
Mishkin... princeling... messiah
Ahab... obsessive... role model
Murakami... surreal... magician
Joseph... servant... teacher
Master of the game of mental marbles
Master of himself
Could any of you show me a way
To see out another day?
A reason not so much to live,
But one not to die
A truth with a small 't' that's not a lie.

Looking up evening fast approaches
Lost in lines time has passed me by
Procrastinating time waster, changeling coward
None of my well-earned titles appeal
But then again none should be denied or ever set aside
They are as real as my dishonesty allows.

Night bends it's crooked finger in my direction
An invitation perhaps
To improvise a further warrant
A grant, or condemnation,
Issued in darkness
By who knows who,
Almost furious, though ultimately resigned
Never to know upon what authority
I am sentenced to fulfil another day.

Sleep and my cocksure, Jackdaw, outlaw companion returns
The familiar flutter of feathers and eyelids heralds
Temporary oblivions blessed approach
Promises a dream
A triumph of hope over experience
That maybe this time I might sleep forever.

A.M. TOMORROW, AGAIN

Waking to the numerous, far too numerous
Oft regrettable, insatiable
Elements that comprise and compromise
The stranger I have become...

DIALOGUES

*Imagined conversations, voices from
literature, history and mythology*

The River, Breath and Stillness
Confucius 551 BCE – 479 BCE
Lao Tzu traditionally 6th century BCE
The Buddha traditionally 563 BCE – 483BCE

The Lantern, the Lens and the Law
Paracelsus: (Swiss physician, philosopher, alchemist, 1493 -1541)
Spinoza: (Jewish, Dutch, rationalist philosopher 1632 -1677)
Newton: (English physicist, mathematician 1642 – 1727)

The Crown and the Grave
(Characters from Shakespeare)
Richard II: (written circa1595)
Julius Caesar: (written circa1599)
Ghost of Hamlet's Father: (written circa1600)

A rebuttal

Bolingbroke (Later Henry IV)
Brutus
Claudius (Hamlet's father's brother)

THE RIVER, BREATH AND STILLNESS

Confucius:
The world is a garden we enter in disrepair.
Order must be planted, ritual watered,
the crooked branches trimmed by the patient hand of the sage.
Reality is a mirror.
Which, if cracked, reflects only chaos.
The Way, for me, is in the rectification of names though tradition.

Lau Tzu:
Ah! Master Kong, you speak of names as though they were real.
But the Dao, the true Dao, cannot be named.
To name is to divide, to divide is to forget.
Reality flows, it does not bow to ceremony,
it cannot be pinned to a moment.
It slips between the fingers, like water, like breath.
What you call disorder,
is only your mind resisting inevitable change.

The Buddha:
Both of you speak from longing,
one for permanence, one for surrender.
But I have seen all that is impermanent,
and that all is impermanent.
Even the self is but a flame dancing in the wind.
Reality is Dukkha, suffering, suffering born of grasping.
We suffer because we believe there is something to hold.

Confucius:
But society must surely be held.
Family, duty, the elder and the youth in their correct order.
These are not illusions; they are the bones upon which civilisation rests.
Without them we fall into animal desire.
Even the sage must eat, must teach, must honour the ancestors.

Lau Tzu:

The ancestors are now mere clouds, let them pass.
They can no longer hear you.
I honour their lives by walking, as the wind walks… gently.
Without resistance, leaving no footprints.
The greatest action is inaction.
The purest form is unformed.
The truest speech is silence.

The Buddha:

Silence yes, but not escape, not indifference.
One must first see clearly.
The origin of suffering is desire.
Desire arises, clings, burns, then vanishes,
to form anew again and again.
Freedom lies not in ritual Master Kong,
nor in the flowing of the world my brother Lau,
but in letting go of the world entirely.

Confucius:

Yet Prince, can one ever let go of the world
without first learning to serve it appropriately?
Even your monks live by rules.
Even the sacred lotus blooms in muddy water.

Lau Tzu:

Let the mud be mud, let the bloom be bloom.
They are, in any case, dependent, each upon the other
as surely as are night and day,
Neither resists the other as they migrate.
Why believe you can bind a river with stone Master Kong?
Why believe you can chain the wind with teachings Prince?

The Buddha:
Because, my friend, the mind, untrained, chases illusion
like a moth, the flame, and suffers his fate.
Freedom is not the lack of a path but the walking of it.
With eyes wide open, feet bare,
heart and mind maintained in disciplined stillness.

Confucius:
So perhaps we are but three voices, possessed of the same yearning.
To live rightly in a world that flows, burns and forgets itself.

Lau Tzu:
But to forget oneself, to shed ambition is to find the Way.
Thus, the tree bends, so it does not have to break.

The Buddha:
And to see the bending, without clinging, that is The Middle Way!
Not ritual, not surrender, but awareness.

Confucius:
Then let awareness guide the hand, and let compassion inform the rule.
For even the river must be crowned with dutiful care in its time

Lau Tzu:
And even the duty must be released, like the first or last breath.

(They continue to sit under a plumtree in blossom, beside the river, in equitable stillness. Three voices, uttering one silence.)

THE LANTERN, THE LENS, AND THE LAW

Paracelsus:
You sit in silence, polishing your lens Spinoza,
grinding the universe into celerity.
But tell me Baruch, what is clarity without fire,
what is ethics without the tremor of the human soul?

Spinoza:
Fire blinds as often as it warms.
And as for the soul, if it exists,
it is merely the mind's idea of a body's existence.
I seek what endures beyond the flickering moment.
To act from reason is to be free.

Paracelsus:
I hear you, yet I have seen base-salt rise from wounds,
and seen the stars bend to the cries of the dying.
Nature is not unmoved, unmoving, she writhes.
She sings in paradox.
And you would reduce her to the geometry of affections.

Spinoza:
Not reduce, reveal!
The man who understands his passions is not their slave.
The mind, in knowing the necessity of all things touches eternity.
I do not seek to chain nature; I walk beside her.

Paracelsus:
And where does your walking lead you philosopher?
To passive acceptance?
To bowing before the iron claw of cause?
While angels weep at the edge of unadministered medicine.

Spinoza:

No angels, only causes only a deeper joy in what is.

Virtue lies in understanding,

not in defying the stars or conjuring spirits.

To know God is to know the world as it inevitably unfolds.

Paracelsus:

You name God as "substance", as infinite extension.

But I have seen Him in a fevered dream, in the burning wound,

in the sudden invitation that defies all reason.

I name God as fire.

As the unseen tincture secreted within the soul of gold.

Spinoza:

Mystery invites awe, but awe isn't ethics.

Ethics is the light by which we cease to flail in the dark.

When a man acts from the essence of his nature, from reason.

He does not fall into virtue, he becomes it.

Paracelsus:

Then all you have achieved Baruch, is to kill wonder.

You have turned the divine into the mere mirror of human thought

But I! I will speak with the wind.

I will gather dew before the dawn,

and mix silver with sulphur to cure the rift that lies deep within.

Spinoza:

Even so your cure depends upon knowledge,

you cannot heal that which you don't understand.

We are not enemies, Theophrastus,

for men approach the same light from different shadows.

Let your fire burn, I will shape its glow through the lens of thought.

Paracelsus:
May your lens never fail and shatter
under the pressure of relentless scrutiny.
Let your clarity not freeze the human heart.
I will roam with my tinctures and dreams.
You may remain rooted in reason,
silent as the divine geometry you so adore.

Spinoza:
And yet here we are, you with your fire,
me, with my glass.
Both in search of the same thing, to live well.
To be.
And to understand what being demands

Paracelsus:
Then let that be our ethic.
To seek… to heal…. to know.
Even when guided by different stars

Spinoza:
Agreed, the universe is one.
but thought like light bends through many prisms.

*(The dialogue fades for a moment, then Newton steps into the circle,
a pocket full of fallen apples and unspoken doubts.)*

Newton:

You speak of ethics as if it were substance or fire.
But what is ethics without law?
I have seen the moon obey gravity's command
as much as the apple does, as sure as breath does.
Quiet as divinity itself.

Paracelsus:

Bah! Another with his head in the stars.
But tell me Isaac, can you distil the soul with your calculus?
Can your laws heal the melancholic heart?
Or the dreams that arise before our bones begin to rot?

Spinoza:

A moment friend Theophrastus, he understands cause,
perhaps more clearly than either of us.
But ethics, Newton, you reduce them to vectors.
Is virtue but a force resolved through angles?

Newton:

Virtue is restraint!
It is the mind's dominion over impulse.
The same force that holds the planets in their courses,
keeps man from veering into chaos.
The universe does not lie, its language is precise.

Paracelsus:

But Isaac, the heart is not a pendulum,
and the will no equation.
You weigh the world but forget the blood.
There is more to the soul than the arc of a comet.

Newton:

And yet the comet returns, predictable… exact.

As does human error, unless governed.

Reason is not a cage Theophrastus,

it is the architect of salvation.

Spinoza:

In this at least then, may we agree?

To understand, is to be free.

Passion can be calculated, not in numbers, but in clarity.

Freedom is not to do as one pleases,

but in acting from the necessity of one's nature.

Paracelsus:

Then you two would chain fire, but I, I ride it,

I listen when it speaks.

Sometimes, the cure is not in proportion,

but in the madness that precedes it.

Newton:

Madness is but misalignment of thoughts, of stars, of humours.

Correct the orbit and peace returns.

Spinoza:

Even so peace must not come from suppression,

but from understanding.

What is aligned must first be observed.

Newton:

Then perhaps we differ only in method,

you, through inward clarity, I, through outward form.

Both seeking harmony, a cosmos in balance.

Paracelsus:

And I seek the spark. That divine agitation.

Let your laws and logic hold.

But do not scorn the whisper of spirit in this alchemist's dreams.

Spinoza:

So, we form a triad.

Lens, Fire, and Law.

Each illuminating a portion of the sacred path.

Newton:

Then let the universe be our cathedral, and reason, our prayer.

Paracelsus:

And mystery our incense.

Let us walk, not in certainty, but in striving.

(These three men beneath the stars, the rational, the mystical, and the mathematical, not agreeing but listening).

THE CROWN AND THE GRAVE

Richard II:

I was once anointed with holy oil.

Not by blood… but by God, or so I believed.

King by right divine, until the throne slipped beneath me.

Like sand fleeing a grasping hand.

Tell me Roman, tell me wraith, what is a crown,

but the fragile ring of men's uncertain belief?

Julius Caesar:

Hah, belief is nothing, without the blade that guards it.

You, Richard, were ruled by symbols, while I ruled by thunder.

The Senate, in fear, crowned me.

For fear holds firmer than sacrament or lineage.

But even fear was not enough, to stay the knives of friends.

Monarchy wears no armour proof enough against

all-consuming envy.

Ghost:

I wore my crown on Denmark's shore, it gleamed,

not with sacred oil, but with the sweat earned in war.

Yet even so, my brother, closer to my heart than friend

poured bitter poison in a receptive ear as I slept.

Crownless in death.

So, I ask you, Emperor, I ask you King, what protects a monarch,

when the throne sits nearer to another's heart than kinship?

Richard II:

Not law, at least, not blood, not God.

I gave up my crown as a man gives up his final breath,

unwilling… helpless.

The hollow metal meant nothing once it left my brow.

Yet still I feel its absence, like a missing limb.

Julius Caesar:

You gave it up, I never would.

Three times they offered me the crown.

Three times I refused and turned my back.

But with every mock refusal I fed their growing hunger.

Even pretence, it seems, is peril itself.

They killed me for the shadow,

reflection of their own limitless ambition.

Ghost:

And mine killed me,

for the prize of irresistible passion.

Serpent in the orchard.

Not so much for blind ambition,

as for inheritance of crown, and a willing widow's bed.

For even family ties, when tempted by power, unravel.

Desire of the crown corrupts blood,

long before it touches the brow.

Richard II:

Then monarchy is naught but theatre,

a part played, passing in fine robes to fanfares.

To be buried at last in rags.

Did I once not say,

"Let us sit upon the ground,

and tell sad stories."

They all end alike… in silence.

Julius Caesar:
But before that silence… glory.
Power sculpted in marble, sung in the streets.
To echo around the seven hills.
I was Rome!
And even though they struck me down,
they could not out-strike my name.
Which even now is better remembered,
with awe and dread, than those of that jealous
clamouring clique.
Is name not a kind of crown that outlasts life itself?

Ghost:
Maybe, but it is not peace, not rest.
You, Julius, speak as men speak who yet live.
But from death we now can clearly see
the eternal flame that consumes all,
all ambition, sanctity, legacy.
Forget not that I too once was King.
Now I am but misprized memory,
trapped within the walls of my son's reluctant vengeance.

Richard II:
Is that truly all we are?
After the ceremony.
After the pomp.
After meaningless circumstance.
Just symbols to daunt the living?
Lessons writ in blood but whispered all too late.

Julius Caesar:
We linger, naught but warnings.
Sign posts on the ruler straight Roman road of tragic history.
Indelibly inked in the language of hubris,
and inescapable downfall.
Even empires end!

Ghost:
Even brotherhood, even flesh.
Ambition sleeps but lightly and never dreams sweet.

Richard II:
Then at the end let us speak plain.
A monarch's power ends when blood and reverence run cold.
And the empire of the worm begins to outlast all our dreams and
schemes.

Julius Caesar:
And where the blade finds its mark.

Ghost:
And where the soul can find no rest...

All:
What then of betrayal?

Richard II:
Betrayal!
A word shaped like a dagger's passionate kiss.
I knew it not in honest battle,
but suffered it in the dishonest silence of council halls.
In the eyes of uncles and cousins, who bowed too deeply.
It is not the sword that undoes a King, but the smile.

Julius Caesar:
And that smile too can be sharpened,
honed to a fine point.
Brutus, my son in spirit, carved my name in infamy.
His blade, like his heart, was the cold of treacherous steel.
It was love turned executioner.
How can one rule, when even affection wears an impenetrable mask.

Ghost:
There is no safeguard against false kin.
In my unsuspecting innocence,
I walked the corridors of Elsinore,
thinking myself beloved.
But a brother's hands move softly,
and the poison came, not in a jewelled goblet,
but in unquestioned trust.
Betrayal is not sudden grown, it is sown in silence,
and nurtured by sideways glances.
It blossoms beneath a palace's perilously polished floor.

Richard II:
I thought my crown a covenant.
I thought divine right was the oath
etched on the bones of steadfast men.
But they all swore to me with hollow hearts.
Even the sacred earth betrayed me cracking beneath my feet
when Bolingbroke returned.
And I, a King became imprisoned.
Guest in my own Kingdom.

Julius Caesar:

The Forum echoed once,
with cheers for triumphant Caesar.
And the blade, betrayal, was not forged by enemy hands,
but by those of sometime allies.
"And you Brutus" my final question.
The last words of the man
who did not fear death in life,
until, at the last, it wore your beloved face.

Ghost:

There can be no treachery without the crown,
and no crown is without treachery,
curling around its form like corroding smoke.
Even Hamlet, my son, knew not whom to trust.
To avenge me was to step into the same shadows
that in the fullness of time killed me.
Betrayal begets betrayal.
It is the inheritance no King dare speak of.

Julius Caesar:

We build empires upon
the ever-shifting sands of supposed loyalty.
Rome for all Her marble, gold, and glory
rests upon that self-same uncertain sand.
The Senate today… the mob tomorrow.
There is nothing permanent in men's hearts, in allegiance.
Only opportunity in disguise.

Richard II:
I ruled by name, but names are such brittle things.
When rivals no longer feared the crow,
they no longer heard me speak.
So that even my own words betrayed me,
declaiming poetry, instead of command.
What is betrayal, you ask?
It is simply the world ceasing to recognise one's voice.

Ghost:
Or your breath, or your body.
They stripped me of life before I knew I had lost it.
My so long beloved Queen mourned with imitation tears.
My once loyal court, echoed with persistent lies.
And all the while all of Denmark smiled,
as my murderer, drank from my cup.

Julius Caesar:
Then the lesson, hard earned, is this:
Do not confuse loyalty with legacy,
Men serve kings, until Kings serve them no longer.

Richard II:
And crowns are worn, until they weigh too heavily.
And then are lifted by another's hand.

Ghost:
And the grave is the only throne,
that none may, or would ever, usurp.
For there, in that final resting place
even betrayal ends.

Julius Caesar:
Et tu…

Richard II:
Usurper…

Ghost:
Poisoner…

All:
Here then, the empire of worms begins
To outlast all our dreams and schemes.
As names once feared… familiar… loved...
Fade to be misremembered.

(Three shadows fall silent.)

———·———

(Three new shadows arise.)

Henry Bolingbroke:
Kings may well mourn betrayal,
but a crown is not forged for mourning!
It is for the bold who take it,
not for the soft who lament its loss.
Richard, thy poetry was its own undoing.
A ruler's voice must be iron, not air.
You complain that the earth cracked beneath thy feet?
Nay, it merely opened readily to receive thee,
in the way that nature claims,
what has grown too weak to hold.
Betrayal is the language of ambition;
and we who rise speak it fluently.

Brutus:
Caesar, thou dost haunt me still,
a spectre of love I cannot reconcile.
But what is betrayal,
when duty calls louder than blood?
In my hand, the blade carved Rome's better future.
Was I not true to her,
even as I faltered in my love for thee?
Say not that affection masks treachery,
say rather that affection demands sacrifice,
and I bore it unwillingly.
My betrayal was no act of hatred,
but of love, misguided you say, yet steadfast.

Claudius:
Oh noble naïve brother, ghost!
Thy lament is the echo of your weakness.
What throne is built on trust alone?
What kingdom stands without cunning?
Yes, my hands moved softly;
such is the necessary way of power.
A cup, a whisper,
these are tools of kings as much as swords and crowns.
Call it betrayal if thou must,
but what is betrayal if not the cost of reigning?
Poison is not the serpent's sin,
it is its strength.

Henry Bolingbroke:
Even though thrones are not graves,
yet every throne leads there.
Still, in life, we wrest meaning from the silence of worms,
turning their quiet into the roar of dominion.
Richard, thou wert the guest of thy weakness,
not my ambition.

Brutus:

Empires rise on fleeting sand,
but some grains of that sand endure.
Rome did not die with Caesar,
nor does the idea of loyalty die with betrayal.
It transforms, as all things do.
If loyalty be a shifting wind,
then we all must learn to sail.

Claudius:

And I would sail the darkest seas of ambition
to grasp what is mine.
No grave speaks of betrayal,
for the dead are beyond such trifles.
Yet in life, betrayal is the crucible of kings,
and those who emerge are stronger for it.
Let the worms have their empire;
while I breathe,
I will rule.

Bolingbroke:

A king's worth is in the taking.

Brutus:

A man's worth is in the giving.

Claudius:

A ruler's worth is in the keeping.

All:

And betrayal, the price of all we seek to hold.

(Darkness and a final silence fall)

James Donaldson lives in Kent, started work in 1969 and
spent 27 years as a chef before going back to school.
He studied for a degree in Traditional Chinese Medicine and
continues to practice acupuncture to this day.

Somewhere along the line he became a philosophical Buddhist.

His has a love of the English language, copywriting, editing
and writing poetry. He enjoys, playing and coaching bowls,
listening to Mozart, Bob Dylan and Leonard Cohen and reading
far too much, if such a thing were possible!

Printed in Dunstable, United Kingdom